Meet My Flowertot Friends

HarperCollins *Children's Books*

Hello!

My name is Fifi-Forget-Me-Not.

I live here,

in Flowertot Garden.

All my Flowertot friends

live here, too.

Would you like to meet them?

Come and meet Bumble.

Bumble is my best friend.

He lives in Honeysuckle House.

That's funny!

Bumble is not at home.

I wonder if he is at the

Flowertot Market?

This is the Flowertot Market.

And this is my friend, Poppy.

Poppy loves to chat
with her friends.
She sells lots of
yummy things to eat.
Bumble is not here!
Perhaps Violet has seen him.

This is Violet.

Violet is quite shy

but she is very kind.

She is also very good

at painting.

Violet lives in Flowertot Cottage
with her best friend,
Primrose.

Hello Primrose!
Primrose always
looks neat and tidy.
She hates mess.

Primrose can be
a bit bossy at times
but she is kind.
She likes to make
pretty things
for her friends.

Once Primrose painted
Bumble's door pink.
Bumble was not very pleased.
He likes his door to be red!

Where is Bumble?
Perhaps Stingo or
Slugsy knows
where he is.

Hello Stingo!
Stingo lives here,
in Apple Tree House.
He sees everything
that happens in the garden
through his telescope.

Hello Slugsy!

Slugsy is Stingo's best friend.

He lives here, in this den.

Stingo shouts when he

wants Slugsy's help.

We have to watch out

when Stingo and Slugsy

are around.

Buttercups and Daisies!
It's time to go home
and you still haven't met
my best friend, Bumble.
Where can he be?

Take me home, please, Mo!
Mo takes me
everywhere I need to go.
I don't know what
I would do without him!

We have to keep

an eye on Pip.

Sometimes Stingo and Slugsy

get him to do silly things.

Pip likes to help
Bumble and me.
We have lots of fun
when Pip is around.

She has the best tea parties

and she always has

a funny story to tell.

But Bumble is not here.

Perhaps he is with Pip.

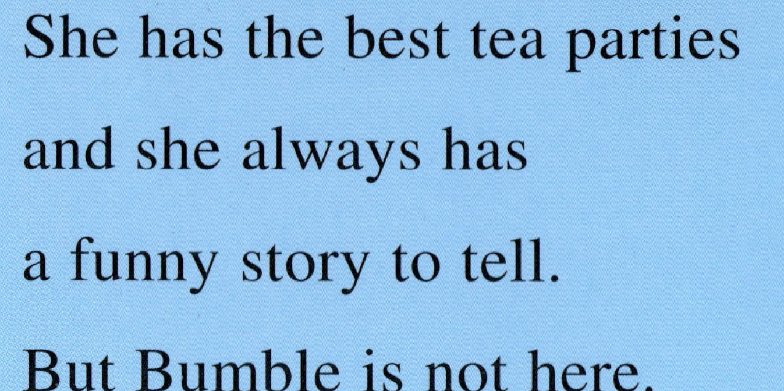

Everyone loves Aunt Tulip
and her pet, Grubby.
Aunt Tulip loves to chatter
with her Flowertot friends.

They get up to lots of tricks.
Slugsy loves Primrose.
He is always trying
to make her happy.

Oh Bumble! There you are!

Where have you been?

A pot of honey! Yummy!

Thank you, Bumble!

Bumble is my very best friend.

He is such a happy little bee!

Which of my Flowertot
friends do you like best?

Fifi and the Flowertots is a magazine aimed at 3-5 year olds who love to be busy, just like Fifi. Join the Flowertot fun in Fifi's world!

Talking Fifi
Forget-Me-Not

Have even more Flowertot fun with these Fifi storybooks!

Fun Time Fifi
Interactive Doll

Magic Bubble Mo

Fun at the Fair
is out on DVD now!

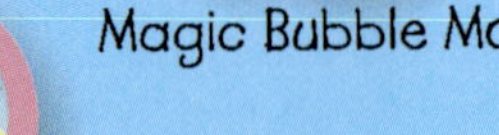

Poppy's Market
Stall & Flowertot
Cottage playsets

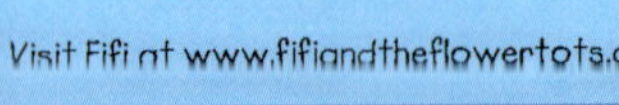